PIANO • VOCAL • GUITAR

BROADWAY songs 4 Kids

ISBN 978-1-61774-043-5

HAL•LEONARD®
CORPORATION
7777 W. BLUEMOUND RD. P.O. BOX 13819 MILWAUKEE, WI 53213

Visit Hal Leonard Online at
www.halleonard.com

BY SONG TITLE

BY SHOW TITLE

BORN TO ENTERTAIN

from RUTHLESS!

Lyric by JOEL PALEY
Music by MARVIN LAIRD

CASTLE ON A CLOUD
from LES MISÉRABLES

Music by CLAUDE-MICHEL SCHÖNBERG
Lyrics by ALAIN BOUBLIL, JEAN-MARC NATEL
and HERBERT KRETZMER

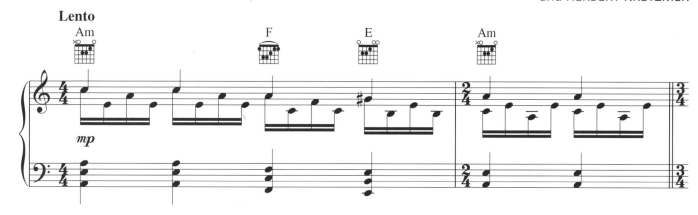

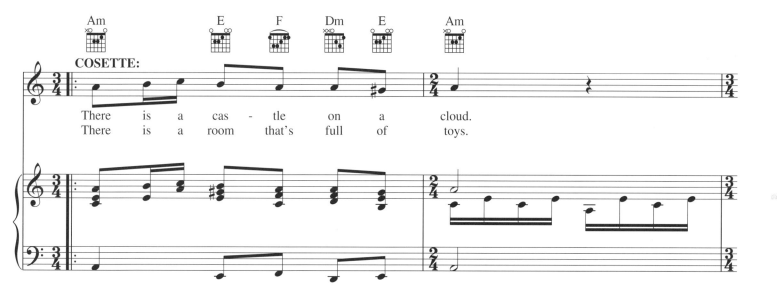

There is a cas - tle on a cloud.
There is a room that's full of toys.

I like to go there in my sleep.
There are a hun - dred boys and girls.

Aren't an - y floors for me to sweep,
No - bod - y shouts or talks too loud,

not in my cas - tle on a cloud.
not in my cas - tle on a

cloud. There is a la - dy all in white, ___

holds me and sings a lull - a - by. She's nice to see and she's soft to touch. She

DITES-MOI
(Tell Me Why)
from SOUTH PACIFIC

Lyrics by OSCAR HAMMERSTEIN II
Music by RICHARD RODGERS

Di - tes - moi _____
Tell me why _____

_ Pour - quoi _____ La vie est bel - le,
_ The sky _____ is filled with mu - sic,

DO-RE-MI
from THE SOUND OF MUSIC

Lyrics by OSCAR HAMMERSTEIN II
Music by RICHARD RODGERS

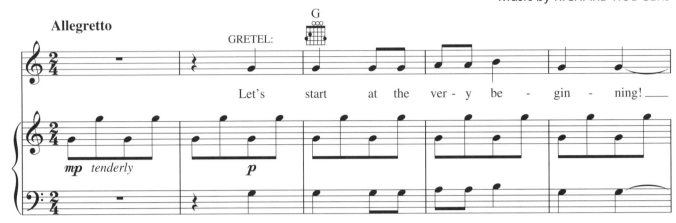

GRETEL: Let's start at the ver-y be-gin-ning!

MARIA: A ver-y good place to start, _____ When you

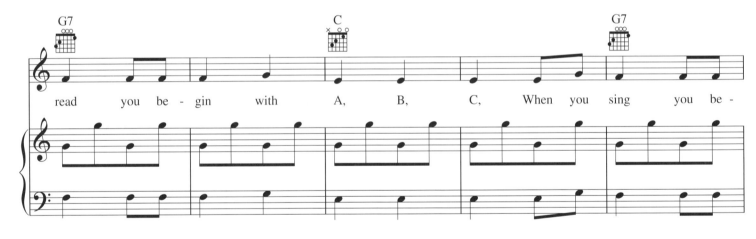

read you be-gin with A, B, C, When you sing you be-

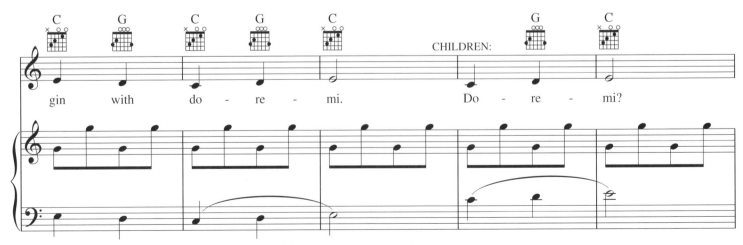

gin with do-re-mi. CHILDREN: Do-re-mi?

ELECTRICITY
from BILLY ELLIOT: THE MUSICAL

Music by ELTON JOHN
Lyrics by LEE HALL

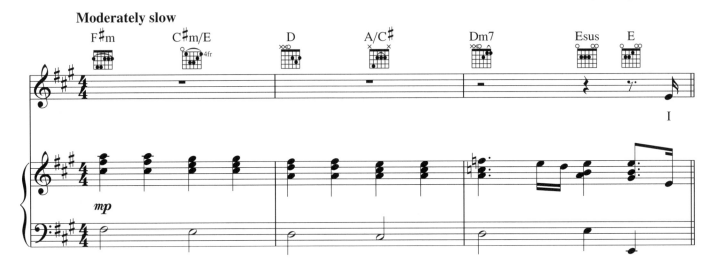

I

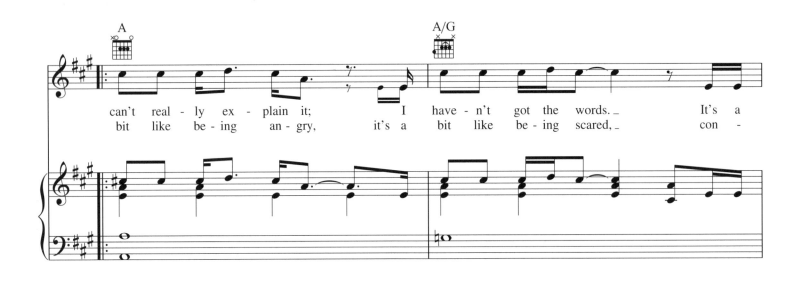

can't real-ly ex-plain it;   I have-n't got the words. _ It's a
bit like be-ing an-gry,   it's a bit like be-ing scared, _ con-

feel-ing that you can't   con-trol. _   I sup-
fused and all mixed up,   and mad as hell. _   It's _

EXPRESSING YOURSELF
from BILLY ELLIOT: THE MUSICAL

Music by ELTON JOHN
Lyrics by LEE HALL

Lyrics:

Is it sin-ful, if you're blue, to cheer up the place? What is wrong with dress-ing up in sat-in and lace? Get some ear-rings, some mas-car-a, heels and a fan; pret-ty soon you will start to feel a dif-f'rent

GETTING TALL

from NINE

Lyrics and Music by
MAURY YESTON

GARY, INDIANA

from Meredith Willson's THE MUSIC MAN

By MEREDITH WILLSON

Soft-Shoe bounce

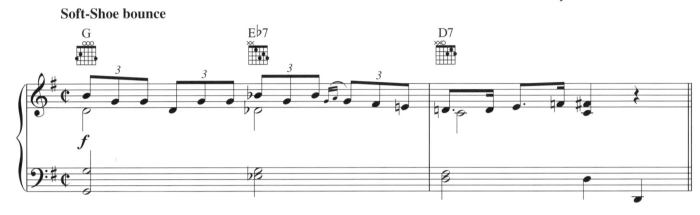

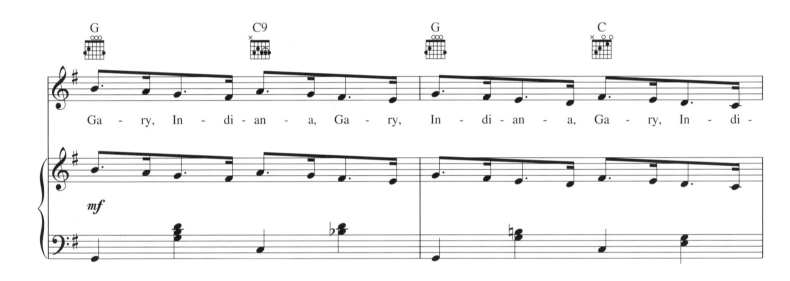

Ga - ry, In - di - an - a, Ga - ry, In - di - an - a, Ga - ry, In - di -

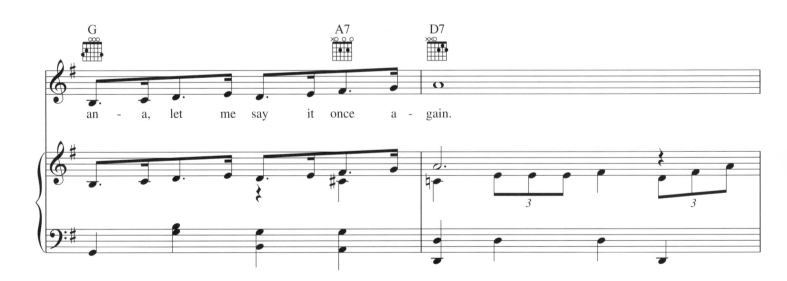

an - a, let me say it once a - gain.

I ALWAYS KNEW
from ANNIE WARBUCKS

Lyric by MARTIN CHARNIN
Music by CHARLES STROUSE
Arranged by MICHAEL DANSICKER

I DON'T NEED ANYTHING BUT YOU

from the Musical Production ANNIE

Lyric by MARTIN CHARNIN
Music by CHARLES STROUSE

I JUST CAN'T WAIT TO BE KING

from Walt Disney's THE LION KING: THE BROADWAY MUSICAL

Music by ELTON JOHN
Lyrics by TIM RICE

think it's time that you and I___ ar - ranged a heart - to - heart.___

Young Nala: *(swing eighths)*

Kings don't need ad - vice___ from lit - tle

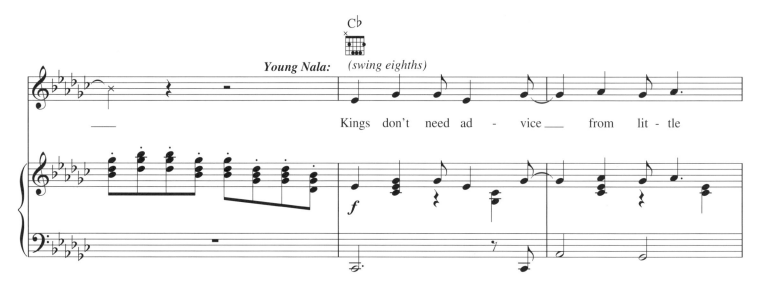

Zazu: *(straight eighths)*

horn - bills for a start.___ If this is where the

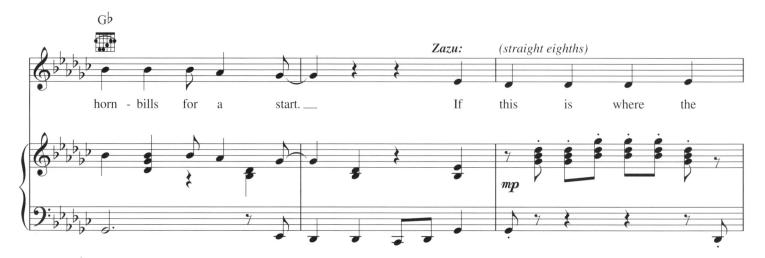

Db **Gb**

wait to be king. ____

G

Ev - 'ry - bod - y

C **Am**

look left.

Young Nala: Ev - 'ry - bod - y look right.

Young Simba: Ev - 'ry - where you

I KNOW THINGS NOW

from INTO THE WOODS

Music and Lyrics by
STEPHEN SONDHEIM

Andante risoluto (♩ = 144)

LITTLE RED RIDINGHOOD: *mf*

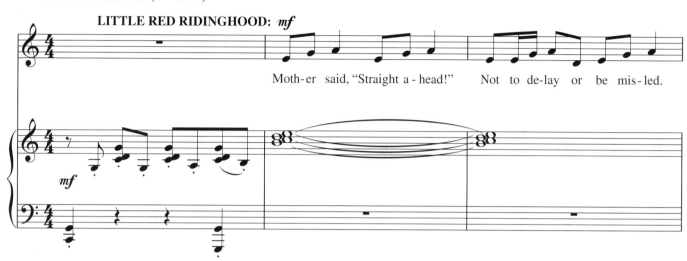

Moth-er said, "Straight a - head!" Not to de-lay or be mis-led.

I should have heed-ed her ad-vice... But he seemed _ so nice.

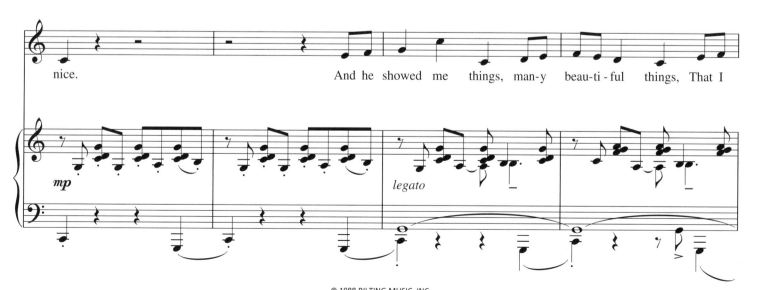

And he showed me things, man-y beau-ti-ful things, That I

I WHISTLE A HAPPY TUNE

from THE KING AND I

Lyrics by OSCAR HAMMERSTEIN II
Music by RICHARD RODGERS

IF MOMMA WAS MARRIED

from GYPSY

Words by STEPHEN SONDHEIM
Music by JULE STYNE

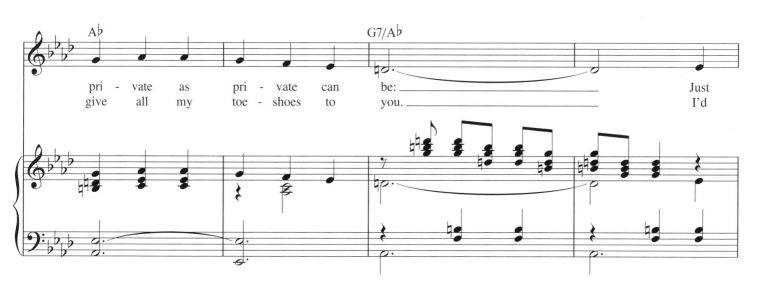

64

I WON'T GROW UP

from PETER PAN

Lyric by CAROLYN LEIGH
Music by MARK CHARLAP

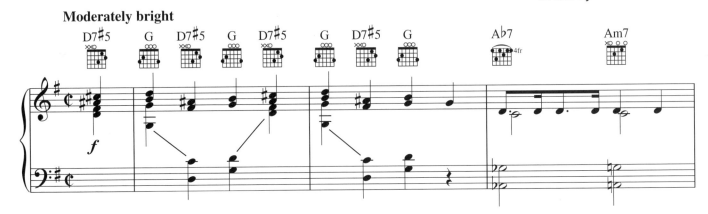

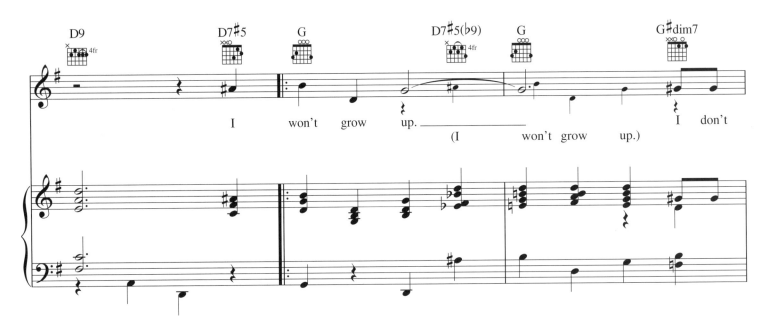

I'D DO ANYTHING
from the Broadway Musical OLIVER!

Words and Music by
LIONEL BART

*1st time Dodger, 2nd time Oliver

IT'S THE HARD-KNOCK LIFE

from the Musical Production ANNIE

Lyric by MARTIN CHARNIN
Music by CHARLES STROUSE

Moderately, with a tough edge

It's the hard - knock life for us! It's the hard - knock life for us!

'Stead - a treat - ed we get tricked. 'Stead - a kiss - es we get kicked.

It's the hard-knock life! Got no folks to speak of, so

LET ME ENTERTAIN YOU
from GYPSY

Words by STEPHEN SONDHEIM
Music by JULE STYNE

LITTLE LAMB
from GYPSY

Words by STEPHEN SONDHEIM
Music by JULE STYNE

LITTLE PEOPLE
from LES MISÉRABLES

Music by CLAUDE-MICHEL SCHÖNBERG
Lyrics by ALAIN BOUBLIL, JEAN-MARC NATEL
Lyrics by HERBERT KRETZMER

THE LONELY GOATHERD
from THE SOUND OF MUSIC

Lyrics by OSCAR HAMMERSTEIN II
Music by RICHARD RODGERS

MAYBE
from the Musical Production ANNIE

Lyric by MARTIN CHARNIN
Music by CHARLES STROUSE

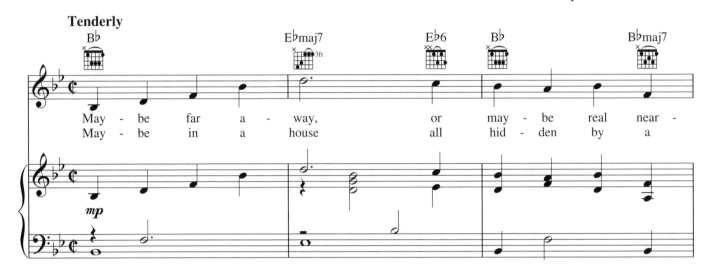

May - be far a - way, or may - be real near -
May - be in a house all hid - den by a

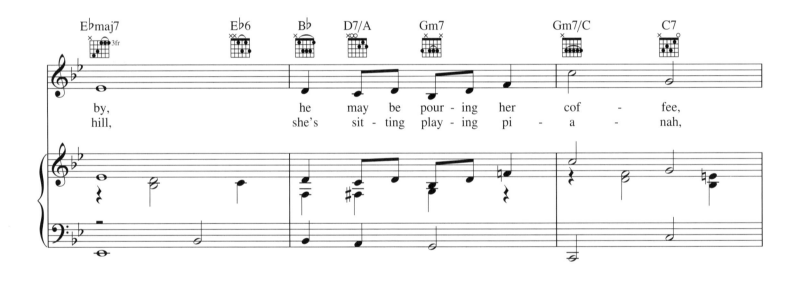

by, he may be pour - ing her cof - fee,
hill, she's sit - ting play - ing pi - a - nah,

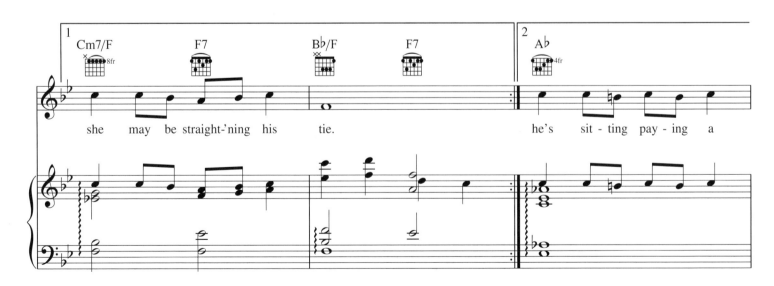

she may be straight-'ning his tie.

he's sit - ting pay - ing a

THE PERFECT NANNY

from Walt Disney's MARY POPPINS

Music and Lyrics by RICHARD M. SHERMAN
and ROBERT B. SHERMAN

MY BEST GIRL
(My Best Beau)
from MAME

Music and Lyric by JERRY HERMAN
Arranged by MICHAEL DANSICKER

Moderate Waltz

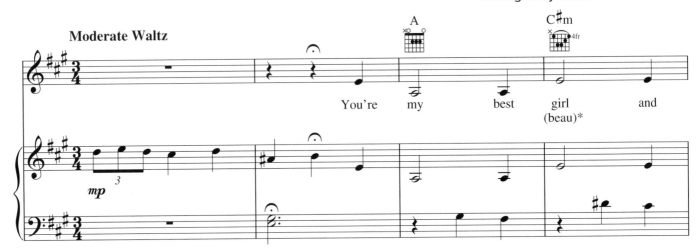

You're my best girl and (beau)*

noth-ing you do is wrong, I'm proud you be-long to

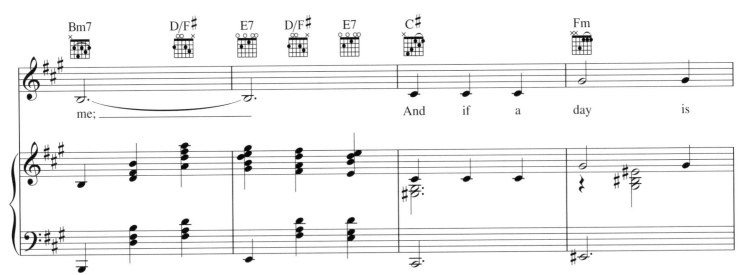

me; ____ And if a day is

*This may be used as a substitute throughout.
This song is performed by Patrick and Mame Dennis in the show, adapted here as a solo.

SO LONG, FAREWELL

from THE SOUND OF MUSIC

Lyrics by OSCAR HAMMERSTEIN II
Music by RICHARD RODGERS

CHILDREN:

There's a

sad sort of clang-ing from the clock in the hall and the bells in the stee-ple,

too, And up in the nurs-'ry an ab-surd lit-tle bird Is pop-ping out to say "coo-

hate to go and miss this pret - ty sight. ___

mf

G7

C

CHILDREN:

So long, fare - well, Auf wie - der - sehn, a - dieu, ___ a -

KURT:

dieu, A - dieu, to yieu and yieu and yieu. ___

G7

mf

CHILDREN:

So long, fare - well, Auf wie - der - sehn, good - bye, __ I

FRIEDRICH:

leave and heave a sigh and say good - bye, __ good - bye. __

Meno mosso

BRIGITTA:

I'm

LOUISA:

glad to go, I can - not tell a lie. __ I flit, I float, I

THE TREE
from THE ME NOBODY KNOWS

Lyric by WILL HOLT
Music by GARY WILLIAM FRIEDMAN

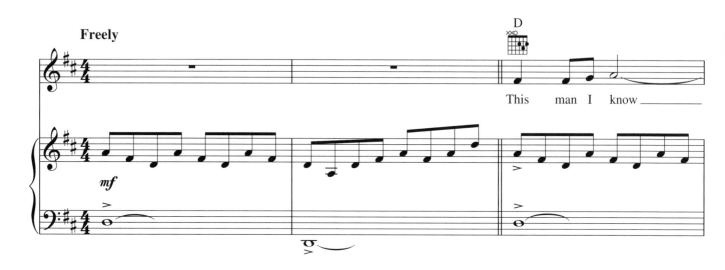

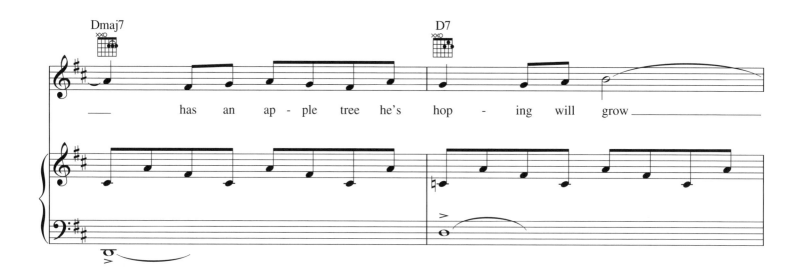

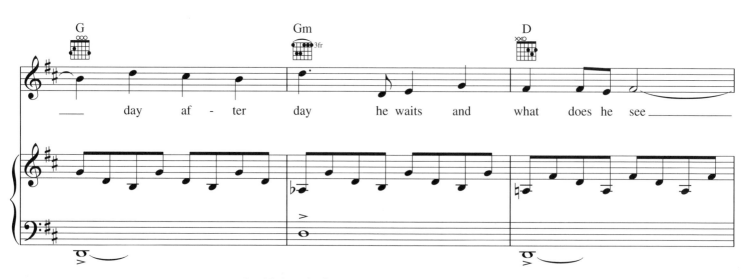

WENDY
from PETER PAN

Lyric by BETTY COMDEN and ADAOLPH GREEN
Music by JULE STYNE

WHAT IF
from THE ADDAMS FAMILY

Music and Lyrics by
ANDREW LIPPA

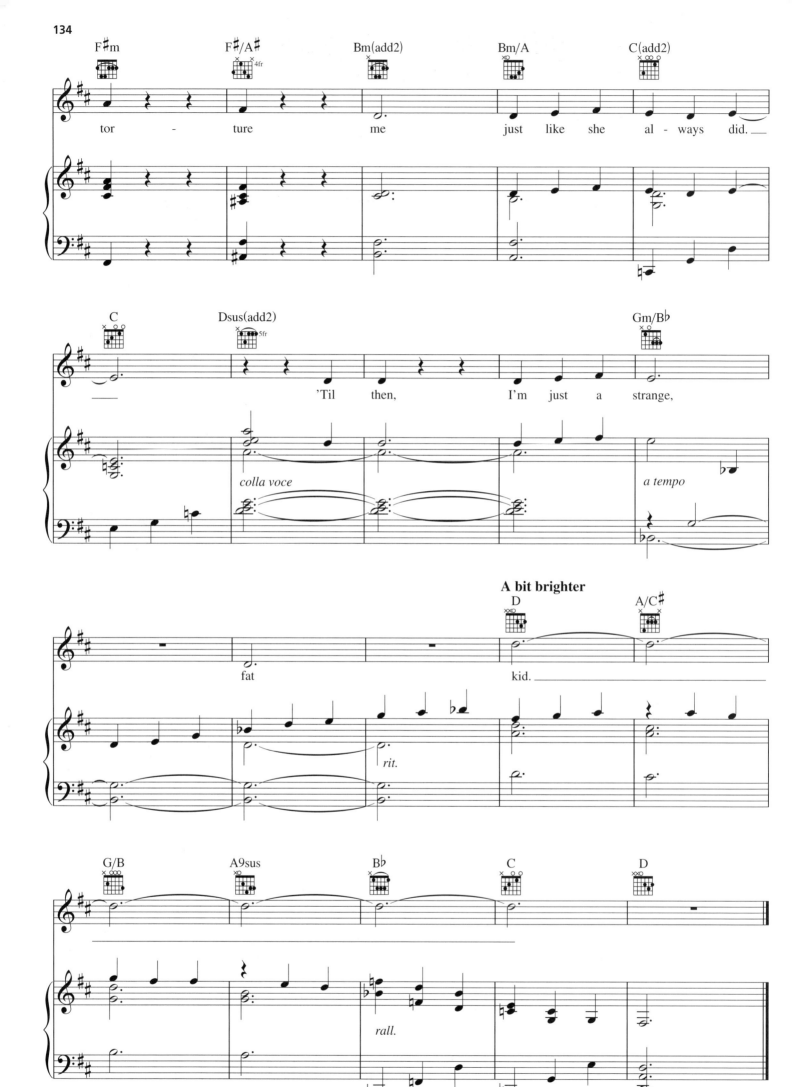

WHERE IS LOVE?

from the Broadway Musical OLIVER!

Words and Music by
LIONEL BART

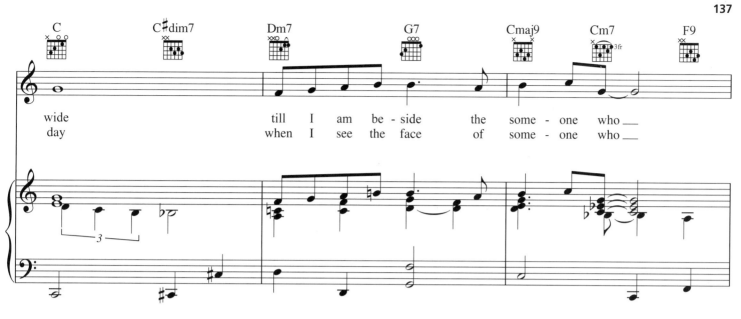

wide   till I am be - side   the   some - one who ___
day   when I see the face   of   some - one who ___

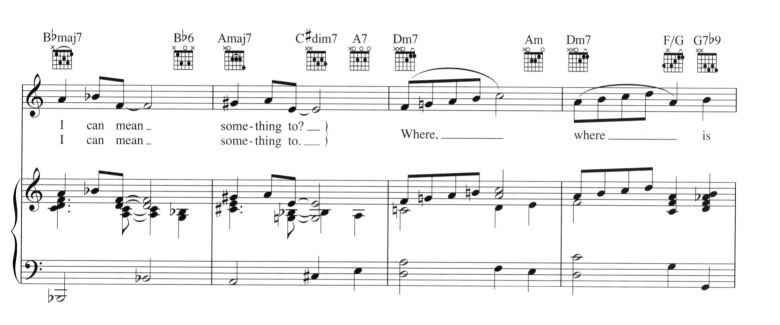

I can mean ___   some - thing to? ___
I can mean ___   some - thing to. ___

Where, _____   where _____ is

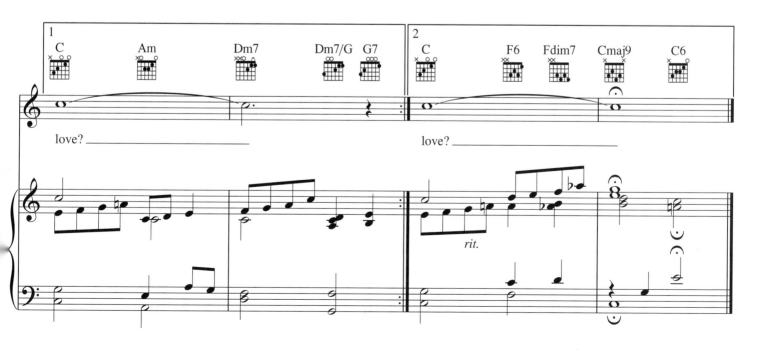

love? _____   love? _____

rit.

WHO WILL BUY?

from the Broadway Musical OLIVER!

Words and Music by
LIONEL BART

YOU'RE NEVER FULLY DRESSED WITHOUT A SMILE

from the Musical Production ANNIE

Lyric by MARTIN CHARNIN
Music by CHARLES STROUSE

WHY AM I ME?
from SHENANDOAH

Lyric by PETER UDELL
Music by GARY GELD